MONEY

Banking

Heather Hammonds

A⁺

Smart Apple Media

This edition first published in 2006 in the United States of America by Smart Apple Media.

Smart Apple Media
2140 Howard Drive West
North Mankato
Minnesota 56003

First published in 2006 by
MACMILLAN EDUCATION AUSTRALIA PTY LTD
627 Chapel Street, South Yarra, Australia 3141

Visit our Web site at www.macmillan.com.au

Associated companies and representatives throughout the world.

Library of Congress Cataloging-in-Publication Data

Hammonds, Heather.
    Banking / by Heather Hammonds.
    p. cm. — (Money)
    ISBN-13: 978-1-58340-783-7
    1. Banks and banking—Juvenile literature. I. Title. II. Money (Smart Apple Media)

HG1609.H36 2006
332.1—dc22   2005057574

Edited by Miriana Dasovic
Text and cover design by Raul Diche
Page layout by Raul Diche
Photo research by Legend Images
Illustrations by Ann Likhovetsky

Printed in USA

Acknowledgments
The author wishes to thank Meredith Begg of Meric Digital for her expert advice.

The author and the publisher are grateful to the following for permission to reproduce copyright material:

Cover photograph: Grandpa helping grandson deposit his savings, courtesy of Australian Picture Library/David Woods; background image courtesy of Photodisc.

AAP Image/Mediakoo, p. 21; Adelaide Bank Ltd, p. 14; ANZ Bank, p. 5 (logo); Australian Picture Library/Corbis, p. 9; Commonwealth of Australia Bank, p. 5 (logo); Comstock, © 2005 JupiterImages Corporation, pp. 16, 18, 19, 25, 26; Getty Images, pp. 7, 23, 24; ROB ELLIOTT/AFP/Getty Images, p. 15; PORNCHAI KITTIWONGSAKUL/ AFP/Getty Images, p. 13; National Australia Bank, p. 5 (logo); Newspix, pp. 27, 29; Newspix, photo by Michelle Kelcey, p. 28; Newspix, photo by Ross Swanborough, p. 20; Photodisc, pp. 3, 6, 12, 32; Photolibrary/A.G.E. Fotostock, p. 4; Photolibrary/Panorama Stock Photo Co., Ltd, p. 5; Photolibrary RF, p. 10; Photolibrary/ Workbook, Inc, p. 22; Queenslanders Credit Union, p. 17; St George Bank Limited, p. 11; SuperStock photo library, p. 30; Westpac Bank, p. 5 (logo).

Contents

Glossary words

When a word is printed in **bold**, you can look up its meaning in the glossary on page 31.

What is a bank?

Banks are businesses that deal in money. Bank customers can **deposit** their money in bank accounts. Customers can also borrow money from banks. This borrowed money is called a bank loan. When customers use the **services** of a bank, they are doing their banking. Banks provide these services for many different customers, including children, adults, and businesses.

Banks use the money that customers deposit in bank accounts to make more money. They lend some of the money to other customers, and charge those customers **interest** for using this money. Banks pay some of the interest to the customers who made deposits. They make a **profit** by keeping the rest.

Banks also **invest** some of their customers' money to make more money. They invest the money in other businesses, both local and overseas.

Customers can do their banking by visiting a bank branch and being served by bank tellers.

Info-plus!

Each country has banks that are owned by organizations in its own country, as well as banks owned by overseas organizations.

Head offices, branches, and agencies

Most banks have head offices, usually in a capital city. The people in charge of running a bank work at its head office. Customers can also do their banking at a bank's head office.

Banks also have branches in many cities, suburbs, and country towns. Bank customers can visit the branch of their bank that is closest to their home, to do their banking. This means that they do not have to travel to the head office of their bank.

Some banks also have agencies. Agencies are other businesses that have an agreement with a bank to provide services for the bank's customers.

The head office of the Industry and Commercial Bank in Beijing, China.

Banking

Banks offer many services to their customers. Some services are for individual customers. This is known as personal banking. Other services are for businesses, or business banking.

Personal banking

Personal bank customers may visit a bank, or bank branch, to do their banking. They may also do their banking over the telephone, on the Internet, or at an **automatic teller machine**, or **ATM**.

   Personal bank customers can deposit money into a bank account or **withdraw** money. They can go to the information desk in a bank to find out about other bank services, such as getting a bank loan or a plastic banking card. People who cannot visit a bank can get this information from the bank's Web site instead.

Customers can visit the information desk at a bank if they have questions.

Info-plus!

Different bank officers are trained to help customers with different banking services, such as taking out a bank loan or investing money.

Business banking

Businesses usually have to do a lot of banking. They may make many deposits and withdrawals each week. Because of this, most banks have accounts especially for businesses.

The banks also provide EFTPOS (Electronic Funds Transfer at Point Of Sale) machines to shops and other businesses that sell **products** to customers. When customers buy products from these shops and businesses, they can use plastic cards to pay for them instead of using cash. An EFTPOS machine reads the customer's card and transfers money from the customer's bank account to the bank account of the shop or businesses.

Many people need to borrow money when they first start a business, to buy the things they need to run it. They can get a business loan from a bank for this purpose. Loans officers at the bank can give them advice and help them choose the right bank loan for their business.

Info-plus!

People who want to start a business can get helpful information from a bank. They can speak to a bank officer at a bank branch, or visit a bank Web site on the Internet.

Loans officers help customers choose the best bank loan for their needs.

The history of banking

Banks have a history that goes back more than 4,000 years. Banks and banking have changed a lot over this time.

Banks in ancient times

The first banks operated in Iraq and Syria, known then as Mesopotamia. These banks were found in temples, palaces, and warehouses. These were safe places to store valuable products.

At first, valuables such as grain, cattle, and farm tools were stored in these ancient banks. Later, the banks were also used to store precious metals, such as gold and silver, as well as coins. People left their products at the bank and were given a **receipt** for them. They could claim their **property** by handing in the receipt. Receipts were also used as money. One person could give their receipt to another person. This other person could then claim the products.

Info-plus!

People were charged an amount of money, or fee, for leaving their valuables with the ancient banks. The banks also gave people loans, just as banks do today.

Temples such as this one were the first banks.

8

Moneychangers

In Italy in the 1200s and 1300s, banks were run by moneychangers. Customers could leave their money with moneychangers and earn interest, or they could pay a fee and get a loan from the moneychangers.

People who traveled to other countries needed foreign money so they could buy products in those countries. When these people returned home, they needed to swap the foreign money for money that was used in their own country. The moneychangers exchanged coins for these customers.

Goldsmiths

In England in the 1400s and 1500s, banks were run by **goldsmiths**. They stored gold and other valuables for customers, and charged a fee for the service. When a person stored gold or other valuables with a goldsmith, they were given a receipt. People used these receipts as money. Goldsmiths also lent gold to people and charged a fee to do this.

A moneychanger of long ago sits in a market square, waiting for customers.

The spread of banks

By the end of the 1700s, banks operated in many countries. In 1782, the first bank in the United States was opened. The first banks in Canada and Australia were opened in 1817.

Info-plus!

The word "bank" comes from the Italian word "banca." This is a bench set up in a place, such as a market square, where moneychangers ran their business.

Bank accounts

Today, banks offer many different types of bank accounts. Customers choose the bank account that suits their needs.

Checking accounts

Checking accounts are bank accounts for everyday use, such as buying products and paying bills, rather than for saving money. Customers have a **check** book for their checking account, as well as a plastic banking card. They can use their card to get money from an ATM, or to pay for products when they are shopping. Money is taken out of their account when they use their card or write a check.

Checking account customers receive regular bank statements from their banks. These statements show the deposits and withdrawals they have made, any fees charged and any interest earned. They also show the amount of money left in the account, known as the balance.

Customers can withdraw money from their checking accounts by writing checks.

Info-plus!

Some checking accounts allow customers over 18 years old to spend more money than they have. The bank lends them the extra money, and charges them interest. This extra spending money is called an overdraft.

Savings accounts

Savings accounts are bank accounts used to save money and earn interest. Some savings accounts pay more interest than others, depending on how much money the customer has in their account and how long they leave their money in it. Other savings accounts offer rewards, or bonuses, to encourage customers to put money into their account. If a customer adds money to their account, or does not withdraw any money within a certain period of time, they may receive extra interest.

Savings accounts for young people

Most banks have special savings accounts for young people. They usually offer rewards such as extra interest for adding money, or for not withdrawing money, each month. Some banks also send their younger customers magazines and give them tips on saving.

This savings account passbook is designed for young people.

Info-plus!

Customers with savings accounts receive regular bank statements. These are generally sent each month, or every three months, just as they are for checking accounts.

Earning interest

When a customer puts money into their bank account, the bank may lend that money to other customers or invest it, to make more money. The bank pays some of the money it makes to the customer as interest.

Banks generally pay compound interest to their customers. Compound interest is interest earned on the money a customer puts into their bank account, plus interest earned on any interest that has already been paid.

Example

Maya's bank account

Maya puts $1000 into a savings account in January. She does not add any further money to it. She earns 5% compound interest on her money, with the interest paid four times a year. Here is how her money grows:

How Maya's money grows

MONTH	INTEREST EARNED	ACCOUNT BALANCE
January	$0.00	$1000.00
March	$12.33	$1012.33
June	$12.62	$1024.95
September	$12.92	$1037.87
December	$13.08	$1050.95
Total interest	$50.95	

Maya earned $50.95 interest on her account in one year.

Bank fees and charges

Banks charge customers bank fees in return for providing banking services. There are several different kinds of bank fees and charges:

- Account-keeping fees. A small fee is charged on most bank accounts, usually once a month, for keeping a bank account open

- Transaction fees. A small fee is often charged every time a customer makes a deposit or withdrawal. Sometimes the bank allows the customer to make a small number of free transactions before charging fees. Deposits or withdrawals made inside the bank generally cost the most. Those made at an ATM, by telephone, or over the Internet usually cost less

- Other bank fees. Other bank fees may be charged for services such as writing checks or providing extra bank statements

- Government **taxes**. Sometimes, bank customers have to pay taxes on their account. The bank takes the tax from the account and pays the money to the government

Info-plus!

Banks generally do not charge fees for customers under 18 years old. Sometimes, bank fees are not charged when customers have more than a certain amount of money in their bank account.

These customers are waiting to make a transaction at their bank.

Banks and investment

Investing is a way of using money to earn more money. Most banks offer several types of **investment** accounts to their customers.

Certificate of deposit accounts

Certificate of deposit accounts are like regular savings accounts, but customers must leave their money in the bank for a set period of time, such as six months. The bank pays the customer interest on the money in the certificate of deposit account. Customers may have the interest paid back into the account, or into another account, or mailed to them as a check. Different certificate of deposit accounts pay more or less interest, depending on how much money the customer invests and for how long the money is invested.

Need to fix something?

Certificate of deposit accounts usually pay more interest than checking accounts.

Managed funds

Bank customers who want to save their money for a long time usually join a managed fund run by their bank. Managed funds are investments made up of many people's money grouped into one fund.

The money invested in managed funds is used to make more money. This is done by buying and selling things of value, such as property and **shares**. Some managed funds also loan money to other banks or to the government.

Customers are paid an income from their fund, which is like interest on a savings account. More or less is paid, depending on how much money the fund makes each year.

Info-plus!

There are many different managed funds, and some earn more money than others. Specially trained bank officers help customers choose the best managed fund for their needs.

These people help to run a managed fund in India.

Electronic banking

Bank customers do not have to visit a bank to do their banking. They can do most of their banking at home, at an ATM, or even from their mobile telephone. These other methods of banking are called electronic banking.

ATMs

ATMs are found outside banks and in other places, such as shopping centres. Bank customers use a plastic banking card to take money from their bank account, swap money between accounts or check how much money is in their account (their account balance). They can also deposit money at some ATMs.

Telephone banking

Bank customers can do some of their banking over the telephone. They can check their account balance, swap money between accounts and order bank statements. Customers can also speak to a bank employee over the telephone if they need help or information about their accounts.

ATMs allow customers to withdraw their money at any time, even when the banks are closed.

Info-plus!

When they are shopping, bank customers can use a banking card to pay for products or withdraw money from their bank account using EFTPOS.

Internet banking

People who have a computer that is connected to the Internet can use Internet banking. This allows them to visit their bank's Web site and do their banking at any time. Internet banking is like other kinds of electronic banking. Customers can use it to check their account balance, pay bills, and swap money between accounts.

Mobile telephone banking

Bank customers can use their mobile telephones to do their telephone banking. Some banks have a service that lets customers pay bills, swap money between accounts, and check their account balance using their mobile telephone screen. Customers receive information from their bank as a text message.

Today, customers can do their banking using a mobile telephone.

Bank loans

A bank loan is an amount of money lent to a customer by a bank. Customers make an agreement with the bank to pay the money back over time. They also pay interest to the bank, as payment for borrowing the money. Before the loan is **approved**, customers must show that they will be able to repay the loan to the bank, with interest. They must give the bank information about how much money they earn, and any **debts** they have.

Student loans

Sometimes, older students need to borrow money to pay for their study expenses. Most banks have special student loans for this purpose. Students repay the loan after they have finished studying.

Personal loans

Banks offer personal loans to customers for many reasons. People often get a personal loan to buy a car. Personal loans can be paid back over several months or several years, depending on how much money is borrowed.

Many people take out a personal loan when buying a car.

Info-plus!

A person must be over 18 years old to get a bank loan.

Mortgages

A mortgage is a loan to buy a house. Mortgages are generally loans for many thousands of dollars. They are usually repaid over a long time, such as 20 or 30 years. When a bank lends a customer money to buy a house, it keeps the papers showing ownership of the house until the customer has repaid the loan. If the customer cannot repay the loan, the bank may sell the house to get its money back.

Credit cards

Credit cards allow customers to borrow money from a bank or other **financial institution**, so that they can buy products or pay bills without cash. The customer pays for the amount borrowed later, when they receive the credit-card statement. The cardholder must then repay the amount, together with interest, in return for using the money.

A mortgage allows people to buy a house and pay for it over a period of time.

Info-plus!

Different loans have different rates of interest. Usually, interest rates on mortgages are much lower than interest rates on credit cards.

How banks make profits

Like any business, a bank must make profits to be successful. Banks make millions of dollars in profits every year. Most banks are owned by people who have bought shares in them. These people are called shareholders. Each year, banks pay some of the profits they earn to their shareholders.

Banks make profits in many different ways:

- Bank fees. Banks make some of their profits by charging customers bank fees

- Lending money. Banks make larger profits from the money that customers deposit in bank accounts. They use this money to give bank loans to other customers, and charge interest on the loans. Banks pay some of the interest to the customers who deposited the money, as payment for using it. They make a profit by keeping the rest of the interest

- Other methods. Banks also make profits by buying other businesses, and investing money in other businesses that make profits

Info-plus!

Banks pay taxes to the government, like any other business.

Shareholders can ask senior bank staff questions during the annual general meeting.

Increasing profits

Banks try to make the highest profits they can, so they can pay their shareholders more money. They do this by:

- increasing bank fees
- closing some bank branches
- providing extra services, such as **insurance**, and charging fees for doing so
- encouraging customers to use electronic banking. This is cheaper for banks because they do not have to pay for the bank building, for services such as electricity and telephones, or for bank tellers to serve their customers

Info-plus!

Banks compete with each other to get more customers. They do this by offering savings accounts that pay the best rates of interest. They also give loans with interest rates that are lower than those charged by competing banks.

Many banks have closed branches to save money and make higher profits for their shareholders.

Bank security

Large amounts of money are stored at banks. Banks also store valuable items for their customers, such as jewellery and important papers. The money and valuables are protected in several different ways.

Bank vaults and safes

At the biggest banks, money and valuables are kept in a bank vault. A bank vault is a room made of concrete and steel, with a special lock on the door. At bank branches, money and valuables are usually kept in a safe. A safe is a large, heavy steel box with a special lock on its door. Bank vaults and safes usually have timers on them. This allows them to be opened only at certain times of the day, when the bank is open.

Safety deposit boxes

Banks can provide their customers with safety deposit boxes, for a fee. Customers can keep jewelry and other valuables in the safety deposit boxes, which are stored in the bank's vault or safe.

Bank vaults keep money and other valuables safe from theft.

Security screens and alarms

Most banks have a metal screen running along the counter where tellers serve customers. If someone tries to rob a bank, a bank teller can press a button to close the screen. They can also turn on an alarm. This lets the police know that the bank is being robbed.

Security cameras

Security cameras record pictures of everyone who goes in and out of a bank. If someone tries to rob a bank, the cameras will record a picture of them. The police will look at the recording to help them identify and find the robber.

Armoured vans

Banks use armoured vans to move money and valuables between branches or to other banks. Armoured vans are made of strong metal and bulletproof glass, so robbers cannot break into them. Guards with weapons watch over the money in these vans.

Info-plus!

Banks use special computer programs to keep banking details safe when customers use Internet banking. If thieves stole these banking details, they could steal money from customers' accounts!

Banks use security devices, such as these screens, to protect themselves against robbery.

Working in a bank

There are many different types of jobs in a bank.

Bank tellers

Bank tellers generally work behind the main desk at a bank, serving bank customers and helping them do their day-to-day banking. They accept deposits and pay out withdrawals. Sometimes bank tellers must count many thousands of dollars in notes and coins! They use a bank computer to record deposits and withdrawals, and to make other changes to customers' accounts.

Bank tellers also do other jobs. These include writing **bank checks** for customers, and offering customers advice about new bank products.

Customer-service officers

Customer-service officers work behind the information desk at a bank. They offer customers advice about their bank accounts. They also help customers choose the bank account that suits their needs best, and open new bank accounts for them.

Bank tellers spend most of their time serving customers.

Bank managers

Bank managers are senior bank employees who are in charge of bank branches. Bank managers are responsible for their bank branch and for the bank employees who work there.

Bank managers have busy jobs. They must make sure that their bank runs well, and that their customers are happy. Each week they must write reports on how their branch is running, help train other bank staff and solve the day-to-day problems that occur. Bank managers also attend meetings with other senior bank employees, and often do further study to make them better at their job.

Many bank managers begin as bank tellers or customer-service officers. Then they do further study and, over time, become bank managers.

Bank managers are responsible for running their bank branches profitably and keeping their customers happy.

Financial planners

Financial planners are specially trained people who help their customers to manage their money. They also help customers to save and invest money for the future.

Many financial planners work for banks. Financial planners meet with bank customers and collect information such as:

- how much money the customer earns
- whether the customer has any savings
- whether the customer has any debts
- the customer's **savings goals**

Financial planners then help customers to work out how much money they can afford to save or invest, and how long it will take them to reach their savings goals.

Financial planners who work for a bank generally visit several of the bank's different branches to see customers. Some financial planners also visit bank customers at home.

Financial planners help customers choose a savings plan that best suits their savings goals.

Info-plus!

Financial planners can work for other financial institutions, as well as banks. Some financial planners also run their own financial-planning business.

Loans officers

Bank loans officers organize bank loans for customers. Loans officers are trained to offer customers advice about different types of bank loans, such as the different types of mortgages available. Loans officers can help customers decide which type of mortgage best suits their needs.

Loans officers also help organize loans for businesses. Loans may be given to people so they can start a new business. Loans are also given to larger businesses for building a new factory or buying new equipment.

Before customers can borrow money from a bank, their loan must be approved. Loans officers collect details from customers, such as how much money they earn and whether they have any other debts. Then they decide if the customer will be able to pay the loan back.

A mobile loans officer can organize a loan for customers by visiting them at home.

Info-plus!

Most loans officers work at bank branches. Some loans officers even travel to customers' homes and organize bank loans for them there.

Other places to bank

Most people do their banking through a bank, but other financial institutions also offer banking services.

Community banks

Community banks offer the same services as bigger banks, but community banks belong to people in a local area. They are often opened in places where bigger banks have closed their branches. People in places such as country towns can join together and invest money to open a community bank.

Community banks help keep jobs and banking services in towns that would otherwise lose them. If a bank branch closes in a small town, the people working at the branch lose their jobs or move away from the town. People living in the town must then travel much further to visit another bank branch.

Community banks are owned by the people who live in a local area.

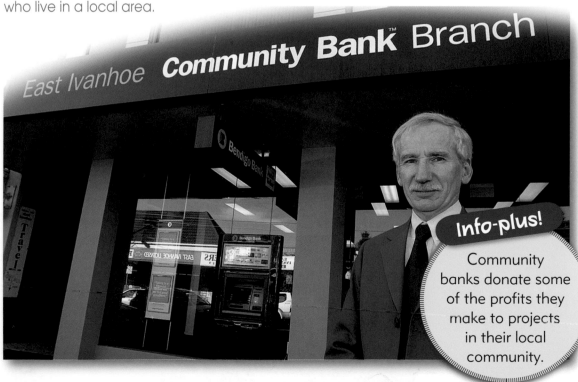

East Ivanhoe **Community Bank**™ Branch

Info-plus!

Community banks donate some of the profits they make to projects in their local community.

Building societies

A building society is an organization that offers the same services as a bank, but is owned by its customers or members. The first building society began in England, in 1775. It was formed by 20 people who each wanted to build a home. Each member of the group invested money in the building society. When all the group members had built a home, the building society was closed.

The idea spread, and soon building societies opened in many countries. Over time, building societies changed, and they did not close after members had built their homes. Today, building societies offer many different banking services.

Credit unions

Like building societies, credit unions offer loans and other banking services to their members. Credit unions are often formed by groups of people, such as police officers and teachers, who work at one type of job. The first credit union was formed by farmers in Germany, in 1864. It was formed to help a group of farmers buy seed and farm equipment.

The Traditional Credit Union was formed to provide banking services to Indigenous people living in areas that are far from towns and cities.

Open your own bank account

You can open your own bank account. Here's how:

1 Ask an adult to take you to a bank. People under 18 years old need an adult's permission to open a bank account.

2 Go to the information desk and see the customer-service officer. Ask about different bank accounts. Most banks have savings accounts especially for young people.

3 Choose the bank account that suits you best. Are you saving for something special, or will you make many deposits and withdrawals?

4 Give your details to the customer-service officer, who will open your new bank account.

5 Go to the bank teller and make your first deposit. You can use a book of forms, called a deposit book, or a special form at the bank.

Info-plus!

Always keep bank statements that are sent to you, because they provide a record of your savings.

Make sure you take an adult with you when opening your own bank account.